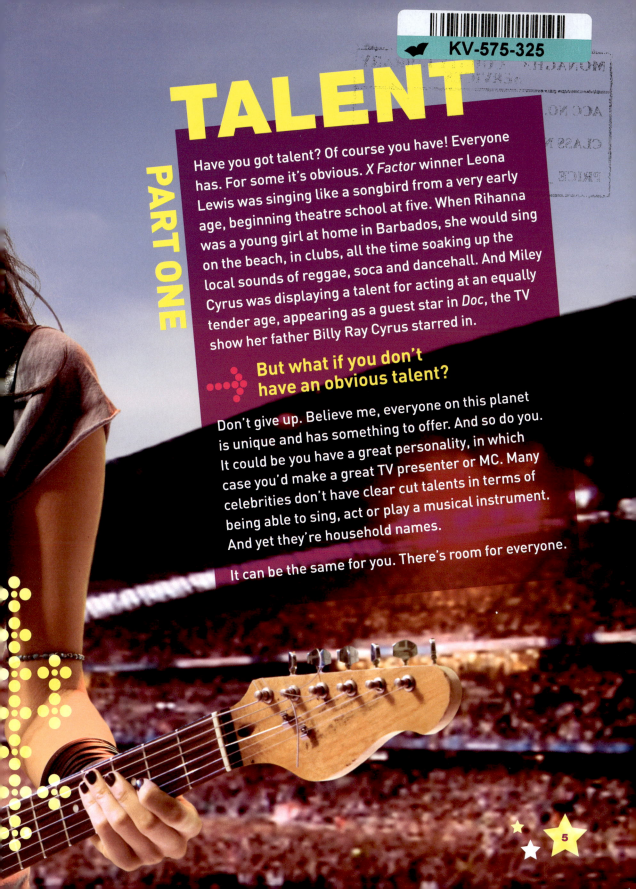

TALENT

Have you got talent? Of course you have! Everyone has. For some it's obvious. *X Factor* winner Leona Lewis was singing like a songbird from a very early age, beginning theatre school at five. When Rihanna was a young girl at home in Barbados, she would sing on the beach, in clubs, all the time soaking up the local sounds of reggae, soca and dancehall. And Miley Cyrus was displaying a talent for acting at an equally tender age, appearing as a guest star in *Doc*, the TV show her father Billy Ray Cyrus starred in.

But what if you don't have an obvious talent?

Don't give up. Believe me, everyone on this planet is unique and has something to offer. And so do you. It could be you have a great personality, in which case you'd make a great TV presenter or MC. Many celebrities don't have clear cut talents in terms of being able to sing, act or play a musical instrument. And yet they're household names.

It can be the same for you. There's room for everyone.

★ SINGING ➤

If you're a natural songbird, and it's a breeze to catch the high notes in "I Will Always Love You" (the Whitney Houston hit), then you can take your gift all the way. What's more, you can gain valuable experience by playing live in clubs and pubs like *X Factor* winner Shayne Ward did before winning the competition in 2005.

You'll need to form or join a band – but joining one should be easy as excellent vocal talents are always in demand. To find other musicians or to join a band, simply put adverts up in your local rehearsal rooms or music shops. Alternatively, use the excellent online classifieds service *Craig's List*. Go to www.craigslist.org and select your country and city or town.

If your pitch isn't quite perfect, you'll need to develop the sound of your voice. Aim to make it distinctive like Duffy, Katy Perry or Gary Lightbody, lead singer of Snow Patrol. All three can sing, but have highly distinctive voices that stand out from the crowd. The key is to work on making your voice expressive and full of

SHAYNE WARD

SNOW PATROL

personality. Make it instantly recognisable. If you can't hold a tune at all, consider rapping like 50 Cent or Eminem. Or develop an unusual vocal sound like the deep raucous rasp of Southern rap star Young Jeezy. Again, you have to work at perfecting the sound of your voice because you're relying on the spoken word to make an impression. Keep up with the latest in rap and hip-hop at www.sixshot.com.

It's also worth bearing in mind that software like *Auto-Tune*, which uses a "phase vocoder", will make your voice sound more in tune. Kanye West, Lil Wayne, Chris Brown, and Akon have all used *Auto-Tune* to good effect. And in 2009 *Time* magazine revealed that *Auto-Tune* had been used to "save" Britney Spears' vocals. Country singer Faith Hill has confessed to using *Auto-Tune* live to "guarantee a good performance".

Find out more at: www.antarestech.com

TOP TIPS

If you've got an Xbox, get karaoke game Lips (Microsoft). It will rate your singing abilities as you sing along to songs like "Mercy" by Duffy and "Young Folks" by Peter Bjorn and John. Go to www.xbox.com/en-US/games/l/lips

SONGWRITING

RIHANNA

When you become a famous singer and recording artist, you'll gain a lot more respect if you write your own songs – certainly in the long run. You'll also make a lot more money. In the music business, the real financial rewards come from songwriters' royalties. The bottom line is: if your song goes to number one in the UK and US charts, the person who wrote it – a professional songwriter or another artist – will earn more money than you do.

In January 2009, Lily Allen told *Q Radio*: "There's no point in going into music if you don't write your own stuff because you're not going to sustain any kind of income – unless you really want to tour, because that's the only way you're going to get any money."

When you pen songs, concentrate on making them catchy and include lots of memorable "hooks". The fuzz guitar riff on Rihanna's "Shut Up and Drive" is a good example of a hook, as is the retro Roland TR-808 drum machine on Kanye West's "Love Lockdown" track (the drum machine was featured on the whole *808s & Heartbreak* album).

Another tip is to make sure your lyrics relate to the lives of your target audience. This will stir people's emotions and make them much more likely to buy your record. Also remember that lyrics that rhyme are more memorable than those that don't.

Writing your own songs is also more likely to bring you a lasting and lucrative career in music, especially if other people record a cover of your song. They'll reap the financial rewards for many years to come.

TOP TIPS

The BBC website *Sold on Song* offers great advice on songwriting. Visit: www.bbc.co.uk/radio2/soldonsong.

ACTING AND TV

Of course, your heart might be set on becoming a movie or TV actor, or presenter, rather than a singer or musician. If so, you'll need to hone your basic talents. Unlike singing, acting is difficult to practise at home as you need others to interact with. But you can certainly read aloud instead. Choose plays – yes, even Shakespeare (it's fun when you get going) – and your favourite novels to read aloud.

It's also worth buying or renting a bunch of DVDs and learning the lines from your favourite movies. Imitate the way your favourite actors deliver their lines and copy their mannerisms. If you can, video your practice sessions. If you haven't got a camcorder, use your webcam. The idea is to watch yourself in action and continually work on improving your skills.

Movies and TV are a visual medium, so you need to get yourself on "celluloid" from the beginning. Eventually, you'll be able to put your best videos on YouTube (www.youtube.com). If they're really good, you might pick up a following and even get discovered.

Joining or starting a local drama group is also a good idea. If you're at school, getting involved in school productions and plays is a must too. Rupert Grint – Ron Weasley in the *Harry Potter* films – appeared regularly in school productions and played *Rumpelstiltskin* in one play. He also joined his local theatre group, Top Hat Stage School.

Getting involved in productions will give you the chance to practise your acting skills with others. If you're shy, it will help bring you out of yourself. But don't worry if you are a little shy, many actors are, but not when they get in front of a camera or on the stage.

RUPERT GRINT

"IF YOU'RE A GIRL BAND OR SINGER, BEING ABLE TO SHAKE YOUR STUFF IS A GIVEN. YOU WON'T SUCCEED WITHOUT IT."

DANCE

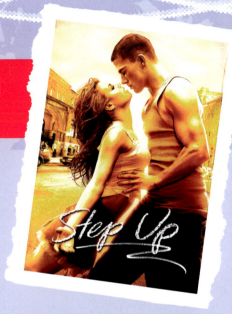

Dancing is another route to fame. Some people have a natural talent for it and are always grooving to the latest sounds. But the fact is, whatever you do in today's entertainment world, you can't afford to have "two left feet". Being able to dance, at least to some degree, is expected. If you're a singer or in a girl band, being able to shake your stuff is a given. You won't succeed without it.

But you can hit the big time just by dancing. George Sampson from Warrington, Cheshire, for example, won the second series of *Britain's Got Talent* in 2008. He put together a great street-dancing routine to Mint Royale's big beat remix of "Singin' in the Rain" and scooped the £100,000 prize. He also got to perform at the prestigious 2008 Royal Variety Performance. The teenager deserved his success too. When his mother could no longer afford to pay for his dancing lessons, he danced on the streets of Manchester to raise the cash to pay for them.

Then there's former fashion model Channing Tatum. He shot to fame when he played a rebellious hip-hop dancer in the 2006 movie *Step Up*. His co-star Jenna Dewan, who played well-to-do Nora Clark, was also propelled to stardom after appearing in the movie. She later won the Teen Choice Award for best dance. As a dancer Jenna has appeared in many music videos by artists including Justin Timberlake, 'N' Sync, Celine Dion, Missy Elliott and Janet Jackson.

To hone your dancing skills, find a good school in your area – and dance every chance you get. Watch all the dance videos you can, and once you've got some good routines together, put them on YouTube!

FAMOUS FOR BEING FAMOUS

These days, of course, you don't need a specific talent to be famous. Your uniqueness as a human being – and an appearance on reality TV! – can be enough. There is nothing wrong with that. After all, those who are "famous for being famous" are entertainers, otherwise the public would never have taken to them. The way to get famous for being famous is to audition for shows like *Big Brother*, dubbed the "godfather of reality shows".

The art of being famous for being famous is to be yourself, but a larger than life version – especially when you audition for a reality show. Charley Uchea, a housemate on *Big Brother* series 8, says: "Personally, I just acted natural. I was just myself. I'm wild and argumentative and I speak loads. I just entered the audition and acted myself. I didn't dress over the top or nothing. I told them I was a South London 'It Girl' and I knew that would get their attention."

Bear in mind that you need to be over 18 to appear on *Big Brother*. If you're younger, consider auditioning for a show like the BBC fantasy adventure show *Raven* or the BBC's *Serious* series where a group of kids are challenged to live in an extreme climate like the Arctic or the desert.

CHARLEY UCHEA

HOW TO SING

★ Breathe from your stomach rather than your chest. Feel those tummy muscles work as you sing. This gives your voice better tone and more power. Look closely at brilliant singers like Taylor Swift and Ne-Yo and you'll see that they sing from their stomachs.

TAYLOR SWIFT

★ Use your mouth correctly. Try exaggerating words, so if you sing "I'm goin' home", make your lips into a really good "O" shape. Notice the difference? Watch *X Factor* winner Alexandra Burke and see how she uses her mouth.

NE-YO

★ Don't strain your voice. Work within your vocal range – no one enjoys listening to a banshee!

ALEXANDRA BURKE

DID YOU KNOW?

Up until *The X Factor*, Alexandra Burke had no professional voice training – even though she started singing at five.

★ Keep fit. Singing takes stamina. The fitter you are, the more energy you'll be able to put into your singing.

★ If you can afford it, go to a vocal coach. Find one at www.musicteachers.co.uk. Or check out the free online singing tutorials at www.vocalist.org.uk.

CASE STUDY:

LEONA LEWIS

A talented toddler, Leona Lewis's musical education started when her parents enrolled her at the Sylvia Young Theatre School, London. She then went on to attend the BRIT School where she took up guitar and piano and began writing her first songs. She started to study opera, but then changed direction and took an interest in singing jazz, blues and pop. She cites Whitney Houston and Mariah Carey as her main influences.

Leona took part in many talent contests as a teen, and after winning several, decided to leave school and pursue her musical career with a vengeance. She had lots of part-time jobs during this time – including working in Pizza Hut as a waitress – and used the money to pay for studio time. "It was about doing my music," she says. "It has always been my passion to be a singer and songwriter."

In 2006, Leona's career still hadn't taken off and she was seriously considering a change of direction. She was about to enrol at university when her boyfriend, Lou, encouraged her to give it one last go and audition for *The X Factor*. She did – and won a landslide victory on 16 December 2006.

Her first single broke a world record when it was downloaded 50,000 times in 30 minutes, and subsequently outsold all the other UK Top 40 singles combined. And the rest, as they say, is history ...

LEONA LEWIS

"IT HAS ALWAYS BEEN MY PASSION TO BE A SINGER AND SONGWRITER."

15

ZAC EFRON

Joining a local drama group and getting involved in school productions is a must for any wannabe actor. This certainly worked for *High School Musical* star Zac Efron. When Zac was 11 his dad spotted his talent and encouraged him to appear in lots of school productions. Zac went on to work in theatres like The Great American Melodrama and Vaudeville. He performed in plays such as *Gypsy, Peter Pan, Little Shop of Horrors,* and *The Music Man.*

At 18, his TV and film career started to take off when talent scouts noticed his ability to wow his audiences. His first roles included parts on American sci-fi drama *Firefly* and *ER.* But the *High School Musical* films made him a worldwide star.

Right now, Efron admits he's a lucky guy to have landed parts in such awesome projects. And he's refreshingly modest about his success.

"I could show you 500 kids in LA, who are my height, weight, hair colour and age. We're a dime a dozen. Why did I get the parts I did? Who knows? But the minute I start thinking it's because I was special, that's when I know I'm in trouble."

Zac also hopes to inspire other stars in the making. He believes the success of *High School Musical* and *Hairspray* – another Efron hit – send out a really positive message. "They tell kids that what's really important in life is following your dreams and truly being yourself. [And] hey, if it happened to me, then, man, it can happen to anybody."

ZAC EFRON

WHAT SORT OF STAR ARE YOU?

QUIZ

1 You and your friends are at a party where there's a karaoke machine playing "Umbrella", do you?
A Grab the mike first and knock 'em dead with your pitch perfect version. **B** Grab the mike and do a good imitation of Rihanna but hit a few duff notes. **C** Grab the mike, but make up for your lack of singing ability by doing some nifty dance moves. **D** Grab the mike and fail miserably to hit the notes – but entertain your friends with your witty interpretation.

2 There's a theatre production of *Romeo and Juliet* at your school/college, do you?
A Audition for the choir, hoping you'll get a solo. **B** Audition for one of the lead roles – you feel completely at home on the stage. **C** Ask if you can help choreograph the show and maybe strut your stuff on stage. **D** Go along to the audition, but be open to any role as long as you can show off a bit.

3 It's your birthday – what would be your dream party? No expense spared!

A Go to see your favourite band/singer live, complete with backstage passes for you and your mates. **B** Hire out the local cinema and watch your fave films, complete with popcorn and all the trimmings. **C** Hire out a hall and a top DJ and dance the night away with your mates. **D** Anything, as long as you're centre of attention! And you have a massive birthday cake.

4 You've won the lottery! How would you spend all that lovely dosh?
A Hire out a recording studio plus top songwriter. There's a hit song with your name on it and you're gonna make sure it's out there. **B** Buy a Beverly Hills pad and hire an agent – there must be a film out there just waiting for you. **C** Hire out a theatre in London's West End and put on a stage production of *Fame*, *Footloose* or *Step Up*, with you in the top role – naturally! **D** Use the money to embark on a crazy venture (such as bungee jumping off Mount Everest!); plus a film crew to record your exploits.

ANSWERS

Mostly A's: Well aren't you the singing sensation. You have the talent and determination to make it big. You could be the next Leona or Ne-Yo.

Mostly B's: Watch out Kate Winslet and Brad Pitt! Your passion for all things dramatic means you could go a long way as an actor. It could be you holding that golden statue in a few years' time.

Mostly C's: Oooh you've got the moves! When you hear a good beat there's no stoppin' those feet. So get those dancing shoes on and boogie on to the stage just like George Sampson did.

Mostly D's: Well hello top TV presenter! You've got the confidence and quick wit to hold an audience's attention. Plus you'll try your hand at most things in the name of entertainment. You could be the next Fearne Cotton or Ant and Dec.

Got a question? Ask Jimmy at www.Jimmyleeshreeve.com

17

IMAGE

PART TWO

The saying "don't judge a book by its cover" doesn't apply in the world of fame. Like it or not, everyone is judged by their appearance, and this applies to girls and guys alike. Fortunately, you don't have to be brimming over with natural good looks. Nor do you have to be glamorous in the traditional sense, otherwise shock rocker Marilyn Manson wouldn't have become an international star. You simply have to make the most of what you are. This involves paying attention to your hair, make-up, clothes and body shape.

Most importantly, you need to develop your own unique look, one that grabs people's attention and holds it. It's no good looking ordinary. You have to look like a star.

CLOTHES

The way to stand out on a low budget is to go for an eclectic look. Buy some clothes from the high street and mix them with accesories picked up at charity or vintage shops, or from eBay. If you've got a sewing machine, you can make some of your own clothes, or adapt those bought from charity or vintage stores.

But as Amie Martin of top fashion title *Love* makes clear, you will have to spend money on shoes and handbags. "You can improvise with accessories, mixing them with high street and vintage shop clothes, and look really glam," she says. "But scrimping on shoes and handbags will be a dead giveaway."

Amie thinks all budding stars should have a good knowledge of fashion. Not just girls, but boys too. "You should create a wish list of your ultimate designer, be it Chloé, Chanel, or whatever," she advises. "The key is to decide what clothes most appeal to you and develop a personal sense of style."

TOP TIPS

- Visit www.Style.com, www.Men.Style.com, www.Vogue.com and www. Net-A-Porter.com for the latest in cool fashions.

MAKE-UP

Don't leave your make-up to chance. Think about how you want to look before applying it. Young girls often think that plastering it on is the right thing to do. But the best rule of thumb is to be subtle.

TOP TIPS

Look like a star! Check out the brilliant make-up video tutorials at www. bylaurenluke.com and www.jemmakidd.com.

Knock 'em dead with the following make-up tips:

★ Exfoliate your lips so your lipstick and lip gloss glides into place. Either rub your lips gently with a toothbrush or coat your lips with Vaseline and then rub them gently with a face cloth or gauze. Before applying lipstick, use a lipliner to line the lips. This stops your lipstick from feathering and brings definition to your lips.

★ Well groomed eyebrows make you look sophisticated. Use tweezers to remove stray hairs. Then use eyebrow powder, one shade lighter than your natural colour, to fill and and shape the brows. Use light feathery strokes.

★ When applying eyeliner, don't draw a thick black line across your eyelids. Instead, work the colour into the roots of your eyelashes – warming the pencil on the back of your hand first. When lining the upper eyelids, look up and apply the eyeliner from underneath the lashes to get a more subtle blended line.

★ Try complementing blue eyes with gold and copper eyeshadows, or even warm-toned purples and blues. Green or hazel eyes will look fab with soft plums, browns or forest greens.

WORKING OUT

Most stars work hard at keeping themselves in shape. Walking, cycling and swimming are great ways to build up the stamina you'll need for performing. But if you're pressed for time (which most stars are) try New York trainer Jay Cardiello's workouts, which are used by rapper 50 Cent and can be done in just five minutes.

Discover more at: www.CardielloFitness.com, or get started with the following exercises:

★ **GET UPS** (named after 50 Cent's song "Get Up"). Lie flat on your back with your legs stretched out in front of you. Stretch your right arm over your head and stand up without using that arm. Then lie back down again without using that arm. Do five get ups with your right hand stretched out and ten with your left.

★ **STABILITY HOLD** Get into a push-up position, keep your legs stretched out and hold this position for 40 seconds. Squeeze your stomach and buttocks in. Do this three times with 40 seconds rest in between.

★ **KICKS** Stand with your back straight. Stretch your arms out in front of you, palms down. Kick one leg in the air so it reaches your palms. Flex your toes so they curl towards your shin. Bring your leg back down. Do six repetitions. Now repeat with the other leg.

50 CENT

BIG IS BEAUTIFUL TOO

Although the world of celebrity is obsessed with being super slim, you can still make it if you're plus size. Former Destiny's Child star Beyoncé always had trouble staying slim. But in the end concluded she's happy the way she is. "I'm very conscious of being a curvy woman and I'm very happy that I'm a curvy woman."

Jordin Sparks used to agonise over her size, especially in school. But on winning *American Idol* in 2007, she became comfortable – and super-confident – as a plus-size star.

JORDIN SPARKS

"I'm really comfortable in my own skin," she says. "I learned that I'm not ever going to be a size 2. I would look so weird as a size 2. Somebody would blow and I would fall right over. It just wouldn't be healthy."

BEYONCÉ

23

CASE STUDY:
NE-YO

NE-YO

didn't give me much," he says, "but he did give me this screwy hairline."

Born in Arkansas as Shaffer C. Smith, Ne-Yo was raised by a single mom in Las Vegas. Money was tight. But his phenomenal success as a singer and songwriter (he's written tunes for Rihanna and Whitney Houston to name but two) means he has the pick of stylish designer suits from the likes of Paul Smith, Tom Ford and Gucci.

The singer, who has had three bestselling albums and a string of hit singles including "Miss Independent", insists he is no blind follower of fashion. "I've always been interested in style, not so much fashion," he says. "I was always the guy going left when everyone was going right."

Ne-Yo (born 1982) is the epitome of style. By day he wears one of his many Kangol newsboy caps. By night it's short-brimmed fedoras, cocked to one side, like his idol Frank Sinatra. Part of the reason Ne-Yo is rarely seen without a hat is because his hair is receding. "My dad

With his most recent album entitled *Year of the Gentleman*, Ne-Yo very much upholds the old-fashioned idea of being a gentleman. "What it is to be a gentleman is inside you – it's your swag, your charisma, your integrity, the way you treat people."

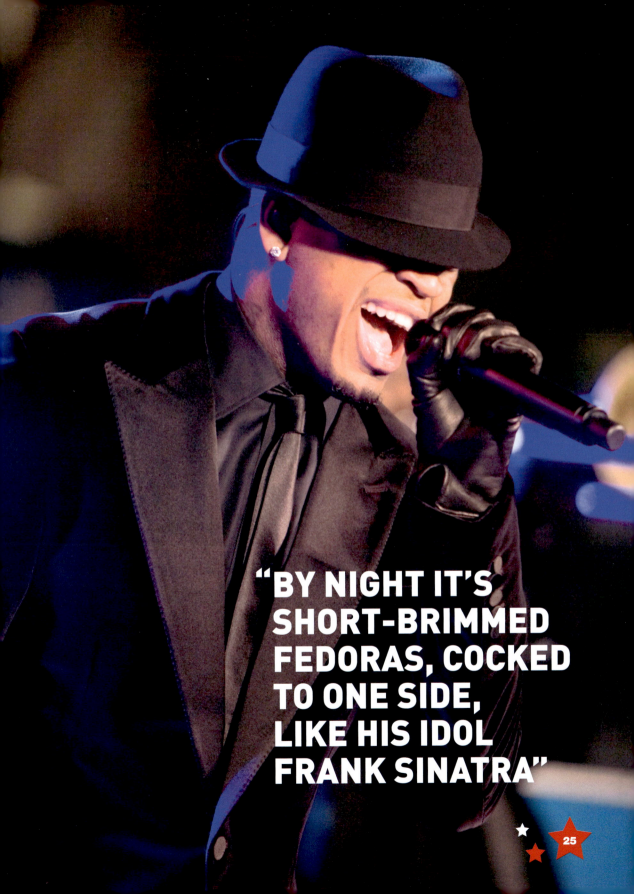

"BY NIGHT IT'S
SHORT-BRIMMED
FEDORAS, COCKED
TO ONE SIDE,
LIKE HIS IDOL
FRANK SINATRA"

DID YOU KNOW?

One of Cheryl's fave designers is flamboyant Italian designer Roberto Cavalli. When she was planning her wedding to Ashley Cole in 2006, her friend, Victoria Beckham, introduced them. Cavalli designed her wedding gown – which apparently cost £110,000. However, not everyone liked the dress. TV style guru Gok Wan branded it "the worst of all time".

CASE STUDY:

CHERYL COLE

One of the most popular fashion icons is Girls Aloud's Cheryl Cole. Cheryl's sense of style has been much admired, particularly since she became a judge on *The X Factor*.

Cheryl has always been happy in front of the camera. She entered beauty contests from a young age and won many titles including the World Star of Future Modelling competition, aged six. At 16, Cheryl auditioned for the Royal Ballet Summer School in London, where she beat over 9,000 others to secure a place. Despite doing well with dancing, Cheryl had a burning desire to be a singer.

So she auditioned for *Popstars: The Rivals* in 2002, singing S Club 7's "Have You Ever".

And while these days Cheryl always looks good, it hasn't always been the case. During London Fashion Week in 2007 Cheryl's style was heavily criticised when she appeared in a pencil skirt, see-through top and black bra.

She also told the *Sun* newspaper: "When I was younger I was a proper chav. I used to love tracksuits. I'd be like, 'Yeah, I got a new trackie.'"

Thankfully things have improved – a lot – since then. With the help of stylist Victoria Adcock – who has also styled Victoria Beckham and Christina Aguilera – Cheryl now wears shift dresses, high-waisted trousers and classic blouses. "She does the ladylike look really well," says Adcock. "But then she can switch to urban jeans, heels and a leather jacket."

Cheryl selects most of her own outfits for appearing on *The X Factor* or at award ceremonies. Her outfits come from A-list designers such as Julien Macdonald and Matthew Williamson. Plus gorgeous shoes and boots from Christian Louboutin and Dolce and Gabbana.

GIRLS ALOUD

CELEBRITIES' NATURAL BEAUTY TIPS

Celebrities might be able to spend thousands on miracle potions and lotions to keep them looking their best. But many believe that the secret of looking great can be found on the cheap in the fridge!

⭐ **CAMERON DIAZ** The *Charlie's Angels* star is said to be a devotee of natural remedies in her lifelong battle against spots. She uses powdered milk as a gentle but effective exfoliant on her skin, which is prone to acne.

⭐ **NICOLE KIDMAN** The flame-haired Australian actress rinses her locks after shampooing in cranberry juice to bring out the red highlights.

⭐ **JENNIFER LOPEZ** The stunning Latin actress and singer has a bargain-buster secret – Vaseline. "You can use Vaseline for loads of things," she says. "From taking off make-up to moisturising knees and elbows."

⭐ **JENNIFER ANISTON** The *Friends* star's beauty secret doesn't cost a penny. "I drink loads of water," she confides. "If I don't drink enough, I dehydrate badly and my skin goes crepey. Water is important."

⭐ **JULIA ROBERTS** These days the *Erin Brockovich* star and busy mother-of-three has little time for a manicure. So she keeps her nails in tip-top condition by soaking them in olive oil. This moisturises nails and helps soften the cuticles too.

⭐ **KEIRA KNIGHTLEY** The *Pirates of the Caribbean* star owes her English rose complexion to a simple skincare routine. She says: "[I] always remove make-up before bed and use witch hazel as a toner."

⭐ **CATHERINE ZETA-JONES** The super glamorous Welsh actress swears by honey as a pure skin treatment to enhance her complexion. She also brushes her teeth with strawberries (a natural whitener) and recently revealed that she washes her hair in beer.

⭐ **CINDY CRAWFORD** The supermodel regularly sprays her face with a milk and water mix to keep her skin well-hydrated (according to experts, milk contains antimicrobial and cleansing properties).

ARE YOU A FASHION ICON IN THE MAKING?

QUIZ

1 Your fave TV programme is?
A *Masterchef*
B *Hollyoaks*
C *Gok's Fashion Fix*

2 You are going to a party – how do you decide what to wear?
A Find out what your friends are wearing and more or less copy.
B Spend ages trawling the high street for something that looks fabulous on you.
C Go to fashion websites like Vogue.com to see what the latest look is, then have a go at making something.

3 What is/was your fave subject at school?
A Science
B English
C Art

4 Which celebs do you most admire?
A Bill Oddie and Kate Humble
B Vanessa Hudgens and Zac Efron
C Cheryl Cole and David Beckham

ANSWERS

Mostly A's:
Ummm – you've a little way to go before you become a fashion leader. But that doesn't mean you can't look good while you work on it. Shop for clothes that look and feel good and if in doubt take a friend – lots of the stars have done this from time to time. Look at Cheryl Cole's earlier attempts before she got a stylist! One more thing: dressing like Bill Oddie is good if you want to be a wildlife show presenter – not so good if you want to be a singer!

Mostly B's:
You're pretty good when it comes to fashion knowledge. You know what suits you and you're prepared to shop till you drop to find that special outfit. You're also observant about what your fave celebs are wearing; after all if the cast of *Hollyoaks* are wearing it who are you to argue?

Mostly C's:
Wow! Move over Victoria Beckham! Outta the way Gok Wan! You're a fashion guru in the making. How you look is a top priority for you and you're certainly no copy cat. You love to stand out from the crowd and make a real statement with your look.

Got a question? **Ask Jimmy at www.Jimmyleeshreeve.com**

RECORD DEAL

PART THREE

If you want global fame and a lasting career in music, you'll need a record deal. A record company will invest in your act and will bring you access to the best producers and sound engineers who will take your music to the next level – that of superstardom.

There are two types of record company: major labels and indie. The four big major labels are: Sony Music Entertainment, Universal Music Group, EMI Music and the Warner Music Group. Between them, they control around 70% of the global music market, and about 85% of music sales in the US.

Within the four majors are lots of smaller labels, known as "imprints". Sony Music Entertainment, for example, owns Epic, RCA and Arista, amongst many others. Universal Music Group has Mercury, Interscope, Island and Def Jam. While EMI Music owns Capitol, Parlophone and Virgin. And the Warner Music Group has Asylum, Atlantic, Elektra and Warner Bros. You'll see these and lots of other label names on your CD covers or in the data readouts on your MP3 files.

SO WHO'S SIGNED TO WHO?

In the Sony Music camp are Leona Lewis, Justin Timberlake, Pink, Beyoncé and the Kings of Leon. In the Universal Music Group stable you'll find Dr Dre, Kanye West, Nelly Furtado and Rihanna. EMI has Lily Allen, Coldplay, Katy Perry and Kylie Minogue. While in the Warner camp are James Blunt, Flo Rida, Madonna and Gnarls Barkley.

Nearly all the big names are signed to major labels. As the name suggests, indie labels are independent from the majors and are a lot smaller. But often indies get wholly or partly swallowed up by the majors or have distribution or other agreements with them.

The kinds of bands you'll find on indie labels include dance act The Prodigy, quirky rockers Franz Ferdinand and blues artist Seasick Steve. All are big names who not only sell a lot of records, but also play major gigs and music festivals.

Although indies aren't as big as major labels, they're still a viable route to success.

JUSTIN TIMBERLAKE

TOP TIPS

Grab a copy of the latest edition of the *Musicians' and Songwriters' Yearbook* (A & C Black), which is brimming with helpful advice for musicians, along with listing music industry contacts. A snip at £14.89!

RECORD A DEMO

Your first step towards getting a recording contract is to record a demo of your music. This doesn't have to cost a fortune and can be done at home using a digital multi-track recorder. With one of these you can record your vocals, keyboards, drums and guitars on separate tracks, then mix them together to create a finished product.

A very good digital multi-track recorder is the Fostex MR-8XL (www.fostex.com), which retails at just under £200. It has built in effects for guitar and mikes and you can connect it to a CD-R burner for making CD master recordings.

Alternatively, you can get music studio software for your PC or Mac. At just under £70, the Steinberg Sequel 2 (steinberg. net) is a great system to start with. It's simple to use and comes complete with lots of loops (sequences of sounds and beats) from various genres of music, including pop, hip-hop, dance and electronic. So you can be up and running in minutes.

But there's more to home recording than simply singing your songs. As musician and recording whizz Robert Courtney (www.MySpace.com/RobertCourtney) points out: "You have to be your own technician, engineer, and producer." With a little time and effort, however, you will soon be creating professional-sounding demos, which will stand you in good stead for getting a recording contract.

KYLIE MINOGUE

SAMPLERS AND DRUM MACHINES

Depending on the type of music you play, you may wish to get a drum machine to build up your backbeats, rhythm and groove. As we've seen, many digital multi-track recorders include drum and other instrument loops as part of the package. But it's good to create your own rhythm tracks on a dedicated machine, as you'll then have many of the skills needed to become a top producer.

If you've got a live drummer, you'll naturally want to record them in action. But if you haven't, or you're rap/hip-hop, dance or electro orientated, you'll want to get the best possible beatbox you can – ideally a drum & bass machine.

If you're on a low budget, go for the Zoom RT-223 drum & bass machine. Priced at just under £30, it has acoustic drum patterns for rock, R&B and funk, and an analogue rhythm machine for techno and hip-hop. Plus an array of bass sounds which can be controlled via the keypads. Otherwise, pick up a Boss DR-670 "Dr Rhythm" drum machine. Priced at around £80, it includes lots of pre-set rhythm patterns and drum samples, along with finger, pick and slap bass sounds.

If you're into hip-hop and rap, try and find a used Akai MPC3000. This drum machine and sampler was the basis of the hip-hop and rap sound for nearly twenty years – and still is.

MARK RONSON

34

Some artists use even older models of drum machine. Kanye West, for example, used an early "rhythm composer" called the Roland TR-808, introduced in 1980, for his fourth studio album *808s & Heartbreak*. He said it brought a more "tribal" drum sound for tracks like "Love Lockdown" and "Heartless".

PUBLICITY PACKAGE

LILY ALLEN

Having promo CDs to give away is only part of it. You'll also need to create a publicity package to go with each CD you send out. This needs to include professional standard photos of you or your band (use a four-megapixel or better digital camera), a biography (keep it short and relevant to the music), reviews you've had from the press or web, and a brief covering letter.

You can send your publicity package and CD to record companies, venues, newspapers and magazines, and to prospective agents and managers.

Once you're happy with the tracks you've recorded on your digital multi-track, choose the best three and burn them on to a CD. This will be your "master recording", which you'll use to run copies from. Look for a CD copying service like www.MediaSourcing.com. They'll run off as many copies as you want from your master recording. If you have a standard jewel case and inlay, you'll be looking at paying a few hundred pounds for 500 copies. But the more copies you get done, the cheaper it gets.

TOP TIPS

Keep costs down, use the free Open Office suite (www.OpenOffice.org) to create your publicity materials. Open Office also has a handy PDF converter which is useful if you need to offer any of your materials for download from the web.

THE INTERNET

Before you consider contacting record companies, you need to generate a buzz around your act. A great place to start is the internet, which has helped propel a number of artists to the top of the charts! The Arctic Monkeys, for example, built up a huge following from their MySpace page. As a result, Domino Records (who also represented Franz Ferdinand) picked them up.

Then there was Sandi Thom whose debut track "I Wish I Was A Punk Rocker" went to number one after she created a massive buzz online. It happened by accident. Sandi's car kept breaking down on the way to gigs, so she decided to broadcast live shows from her South London basement via a webcam. After two weeks she picked up an audience of 162,000 – bigger than Wembley Stadium!

And we mustn't forget Lily Allen who put four songs on her MySpace page, and quickly picked up 25,000 friends – not to mention a huge amount of advance interest in her debut album *Alright Still*.

Setting up a MySpace (www.MySpace.com) page is a must. It brings you access to over 100 million users, some of whom are bound to like your act. Not only can you feature your songs and photos, but you can also announce live dates, new releases, and any other news you have. If you enjoy writing you can also post regularly to your MySpace blog – like Lily Allen does.

SANDI THOM

You should also set up a Facebook page. Bands are only allowed to set up a Facebook "page". But if you join as an individual, you can set up an "account", which makes it easy to interact with friends and fans alike. You can also set up a Facebook group where people can talk about you and your music.

Joining Twitter (www.Twitter.com) is also worthwhile. It has around 10 million users and is growing all the time.

Ideally, you should also set up your own website with a domain name like "MyBand.com" or "MyName.com".

You can register domains at www.123-Reg.co.uk. Each domain name costs about £10 a year. You also need hosting for your domain name to point to.

TOP TIPS

Use Ping.fm to manage all your social networking from one place. When you write status updates and blogs on Ping.fm, they'll be syndicated to MySpace, Twitter, Bebo and Facebook.

One of the very best hosting providers in the world is Hostica.com. It's technical support is excellent and you can run a website for around £30 a year.

Once you've set up a website you can plug in www.WordPress.org, which is a free blog engine that makes it very easy to create and run a website. Many popular sites are powered by WordPress.

It goes without saying that you should link to all your social networking pages from your website, and vice versa. You can also sell your music directly from your site, either as MP3 downloads or as CDs by mail-order.

PLAYING LIVE

You definitely need to play live. It will hone your act and is a key part of building up a following – not to mention getting a record deal. You can also sell CDs, t-shirts, and other merchandise at live dates. If you're performing your own songs you'll typically have to play for free until you build up a solid fan base. Once you've got that you'll get paid a percentage of the door takings. It's also crucial to play regular dates in London as this is where most record company talent-scouts and other music business insiders hang out.

But if you can put together a set of cover versions, you can make a good living playing pubs, clubs, weddings and corporate events.

Don't forget the summer festivals. If you're an unsigned band you can't expect to play Glastonbury or Reading, but there are lots of other festivals you should consider approaching to play at. It all gets your name known and is part of the process of becoming famous.

KATY PERRY

TOP TIPS

If you're already playing live in pubs and clubs, you'll get better-paying gigs if you have an agent. To find one visit www.entsweb.co.uk.

A&R

Now that you have everything in place, it's time to go for a record deal. Your first task is to attract the attentions of A&R (Artists & Repertoire) talent scouts. Their job within a record company is to find new artists who, hopefully, will make hit records for years to come.

A&R scouts listen to demos, go to gigs and generally stay on the pulse of the music scene looking for the next big thing (hopefully you).

The bottom line is: A&R won't consider a band or singer who hasn't already made their presence known on the music scene. So it's crucial that you play live and promote yourself over the internet.

Once you've got that in hand, you should send your demo and publicity package to A&R departments. Ideally, you'll get the name of the A&R person most likely to be interested in your style of music, and send your package directly to them.

Another way to attract the attentions of A&R talent scouts is to get your "white label" CD or MP3 played in clubs. This is a great route to follow if you're a dance, hip-hop or electro outfit. "White label" simply means any song or recording that isn't issued by a record company. White labels are typically distributed to DJs and smaller independent record stores as promotional tools to test the market. If your white label takes off in clubs and on pirate or community radio, there's a good chance A&R scouts will come to you.

TOP TIPS

For a list of A&R and other record company contacts, get a copy of *The Unsigned Guide* from www.TheUnsignedGuide.com. If you're in the USA, grab a subscription to the A&R Registry at www.MusicRegistry.com.

THE DEAL

Now comes the critical part – the deal.

Fortunately, you can get free legal advice from the Musicians Union (www.MusiciansUnion.org.uk) as part of the annual subscription (currently £155 per year, or £75 per year if you're in full-time education). Ask anyone in the music business and they'll say joining the Musicians Union (MU) is a must. Leeds-band the Pigeon Detectives, for example, said they joined the MU because "the Kaiser Chiefs told us to."

If you're unsure on anything, the MU are there to help – especially when it comes to signing contracts.

When you sign a recording contract you will be paid an advance. This is set against future earnings. In other words, you have to pay it back out of the royalties you get from music sales. So even if you've got a record in the top ten, and the money is coming in, you won't see any of it until the record company's advance has been recouped.

But if all goes well, you'll eventually be receiving regular royalty cheques and these will make up a sizeable part of your income. Depending on the contract, you will generally get between 10 and 20 per cent of the wholesale price of all CDs sold. The wholesale price is the price shops pay for the CD, not that paid by the customer. The record company also makes a deduction to cover packaging costs (album cover, sleeve notes, label, etc).

If you write your own songs, you will also get what is known as "mechanical"

KAISER CHIEFS

royalties, which amount to around 8.5 per cent of the wholesale price of a CD. But if you're signed to a music publishing company, as many songwriters are, they will want their cut too. You will also get mechanical royalties if one of your songs is used in a TV programme or movie, or in a big TV ad. Mechanical royalties are paid to collections organisations like the Mechanical Copyright Protection Society (www.PRSForMusic.com) who then distribute the monies to songwriters and publishers.

You also get royalties every time your music is played on the radio, TV or in public in bars, restaurants or shops. This is collected and paid to you by the Performing Rights Society, also at www.PRSForMusic.com.

The bottom line is: you will make far more money in the music business if you write your own material. Kylie Minogue, for example, doesn't make anywhere near as much money from music as U2, who write their own songs.

CASE STUDY:

★ TAYLOR SWIFT

Like Lily Allen, Taylor has a MySpace site where she was the most searched for musical artist in 2008.

Growing up on a Christmas-tree farm in Pennsylvania, Taylor spent her days writing poetry and stories and listening to her favourite country music stars, like Patsy Cline and Dolly Parton. She set her heart on becoming a country singer from an early age, and pestered her parents relentlessly to take her to Nashville, the home of country music.

When Taylor Swift was in the womb, her mum used to listen to Def Leppard. Her grandmother was an opera singer. But did this influence Taylor's musical tastes? Probably not. Taylor is now one of America's hottest country/pop singers. She sings, she plays guitar and she writes her own songs. At the age of only 19 she has already made two albums. The first, *Taylor Swift*, topped the American country music charts in 2006. Then in 2008 she released *Fearless*, which shot to number one in the American Billboard 200 chart.

"We've got to go to Nashville," Taylor would say. "Can we go to Nashville? Can we go on a trip to Nashville, like now?" Every conversation led to the same thing. "So how was your day at school today, Taylor?", her mum would ask. "Great. Can we go to Nashville?" came Taylor's reply.

Her parents finally took her to Nashville when she was 11. Taylor took a demo tape of her singing along to karaoke songs. She handed it to all the record companies on Music Row (Nashville's music district). None signed her.

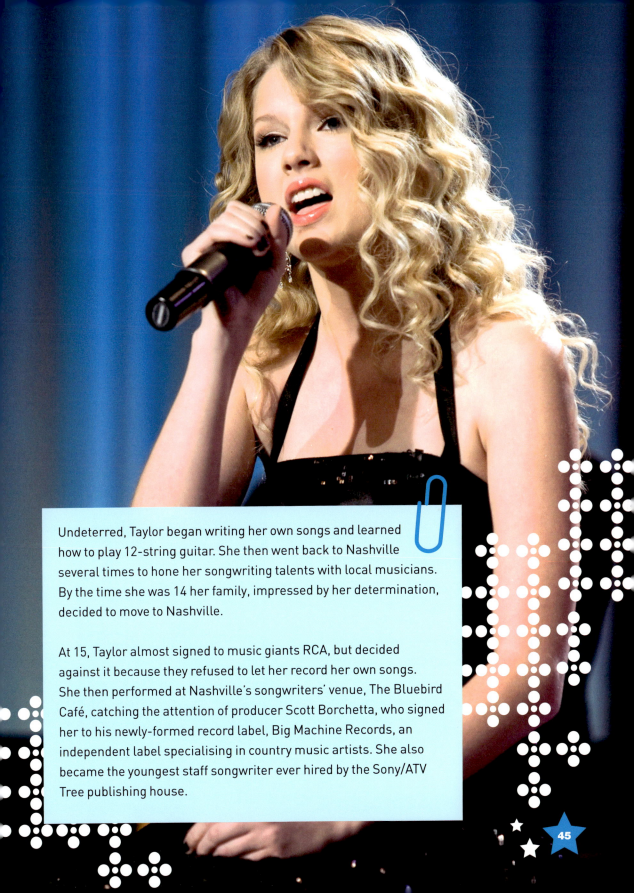

Undeterred, Taylor began writing her own songs and learned how to play 12-string guitar. She then went back to Nashville several times to hone her songwriting talents with local musicians. By the time she was 14 her family, impressed by her determination, decided to move to Nashville.

At 15, Taylor almost signed to music giants RCA, but decided against it because they refused to let her record her own songs. She then performed at Nashville's songwriters' venue, The Bluebird Café, catching the attention of producer Scott Borchetta, who signed her to his newly-formed record label, Big Machine Records, an independent label specialising in country music artists. She also became the youngest staff songwriter ever hired by the Sony/ATV Tree publishing house.

CASE STUDY:
LILY ALLEN

Lily Allen burst on to the music scene big time in 2006 when her first number one single "Smile" made her a star. But she worked hard to get there. Lily was born in 1985 in London. Her dad is actor Keith Allen and her mum Alison Owen (a film producer). Her parents divorced when she was young. She says she had an unconventional upbringing and that she was an angry, boisterous child whose only talent was singing:

"I was really rubbish at school. I had quite a turbulent upbringing. It was middle-class and everything was quite comfortable, but everyone was mental. I used to be really envious of those kids who could do their homework and bring it in on time and were organised," she says.

Lily attended no less than thirteen schools before leaving, at 15, to try to make it in the music industry. She also dabbled with becoming a florist, and an actress (she had a bit part in her mum's film *Elizabeth*). She got her first record deal in 2002, with Warner Music, who thought she would make a good folk singer. Lily had other ideas ...

In the next few years Lily worked on her songwriting but was frustrated by the slow pace of the music industry and began to post demos of her songs on her MySpace page, attracting thousands of listeners .

Her second album *It's Not Me It's You* was released in February 2009 – again she used her MySpace page to get feedback and tempt fans with snippets of songs on the album.

LILY ALLEN

WHAT ARE YOUR CHANCES OF GETTING A RECORD DEAL?

QUIZ

1 Have you got your own website/MySpace page?

A No

B Yes

C Yes and I keep it updated.

2 You think it's about time the world heard your music, so do you?

A Knock out a quick demo and post it to every single record company.

B Get your live act together and advertise by all means possible (posters, email, MySpace etc) and when you feel ready send out invites to select A&R people.

C All of the above plus you'll find out what labels would go for your music – getting a name to send it to and ringing up later to see what they think.

3 How do you take criticism?

A I don't.

B Not very well – but I'm prepared to listen.

C If it's from someone who knows about music I'm all ears.

4 Would you be happy to approach people other than record companies – i.e. DJs, producers, music lawyers, music publishers?

A No way, the record company is where it's at.

B Hmm maybe, tell me more.

C Hell, yes! There are plenty of avenues to explore and these guys may be able to offer good advice or recommend me to a record company.

ANSWERS

Mostly A's:

Hmm, maybe you need to research things a little more; getting a record deal can involve a lot of hard work and determination. If you just rely on sending a demo to a record company you could be disappointed and give up on your dream. Hundreds of unsolicited demos are sent in every week to record companies, many of which are never listened to. Go explore!

Mostly B's:

Well you're certainly not afraid to work at it, but you need to focus and be prepared to listen to those in the know. Lots of musicians have faced criticism but have got there in the end. Don't be disappointed if you don't hear from the A&R immediately, they are busy people and get around a lot of artists. And remember, lots of artists/bands were rejected many times before getting a deal! Look at Taylor Swift, rejected at 11 – mega star at 19!

Mostly C's:

Now you're well and truly on course for that record deal. You've got the drive and you're all ears when it comes to taking on board advice and exploring the possibilities. That's how Lily Allen and the Arctic Monkeys got there.

Got a question? **Ask Jimmy at www.Jimmyleeshreeve.com**

47

TV, MOVIES & DANCE

Getting famous is all about being seen, preferably by millions of people. One of the best ways to achieve this is to appear on TV. Getting on television isn't hard. Yet many see it as a dream that could never happen to them. Nothing could be further from the truth. So long as you know what to do, the right doors can be opened.

Most of the programmes you see on TV are made by outside production companies, not by the broadcasters themselves. Take note of the credits on shows on the BBC, ITV, Channel 4, Five, and Sky. You'll see a lot of them are made by companies like Tiger Aspect (www.tigeraspect.co.uk) and Angel Eye (www.angeleye.co.uk).

PART FOUR

49

GETTING ON TV

Therefore, if you want to get on TV, you'll need to target production companies. Visit their websites and you'll find many are looking for people to take part in their shows. Endemol UK (www.endemoluk. com), for example, which makes *Big Brother*, *Gok's Fashion Fix* and *Snog, Marry, Avoid*, is always on the look out for people to be on its programmes. To register, go to www.beonendemolshows. co.uk. (These shows are for 18-plus. If you're under that head over to the CBBC website and check out the the requirements for the *Best of Friends* gameshow and *Raven*).

You can also sign up with Endemol as an expert. If you happen to know all there is to know about UFOs, you could find yourself on one of the paranormal shows that run on the various satellite and digital channels. Or if you're a parkour whizz, leaping from building to building, you could find yourself at the heart of a documentary on the subject.

Remember that celebrity chef Jamie Oliver got his first big TV break as an expert. A documentary was being made about the River Café in London, where Jamie was working. Quite a bit of footage was shot of the "cheeky kid" who was so enthusiastic about cooking. Much of it was included in the final edit.

"The day after the programme was shown," says Jamie, "I got calls from five production companies all wanting to talk about a possible show. I couldn't believe it and thought it was my mates winding me up!"

Here's a small selection of other TV production companies to check out:

JAMIE OLIVER

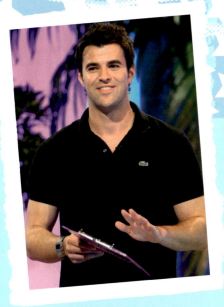

STEVE JONES

And here's a list of "wannabe on TV" pages from broadcasters:

★ **BBC**: www.bbc.co.uk/showsandtours
★ **ITV**: www.itv.com/beontv
★ **Channel 4**: www.channel4.com/microsites/T/takepart
★ **Five**: www.five.tv/wanttobeontv
★ **UKTV**: http://tinyurl.com/dedvap

★ **RDF Television** (www.rdftelevision.com): *The Truth About Beauty*, *Shipwrecked: Battle of the Islands*, *Rock School*, *Don't Forget the Lyrics*.
★ **RDF USA** (www.rdfusa.com): *Wife Swap*, *How to Look Good Naked*, *Dance Machine*, *Ice-T's Rap School*.
★ **Twofour Broadcast** (www.twofour-broadcast.com): *Are You Smarter than a 10-Year Old?* and *The Truth About Beauty*, among other shows.

Appearing in the kind of shows mentioned above is about getting your face on TV and getting some experience of the whole process. With luck, this could lead to you being discovered like Jamie Oliver was.

TOP TIPS

Check out www. BeOnScreen.com for lists of shows that currently need participants. You can either register free for "casual" membership or pay £9.99 a year for "serious" membership.

GOK WAN

EXTRAS AND ACTING

Another way into TV (and also movies) is to work as an extra, or supporting artiste, which typically involves being in crowd scenes. You don't speak, but you will catch a glimpse of yourself when the programme or movie is screened. It's good fun and you'll get a real insight into how TV programmes and movies are made. But be warned: extra work involves a lot of hanging about. The upside is you will make new friends and be well fed (location caterers have a reputation for providing yummy food!).

There's no minimum age for being an extra. But if you're under 16, you'll need your parents' permission and your mum or dad may need to go with you on some jobs.

Here are a few reputable agencies who find work for supporting artistes:

★ www.castingcollective.co.uk
★ www.guysanddollscasting.com
★ www.maddogcasting.com
★ www.rayknight.co.uk

Whenever they get you work – such as on shows like *Eastenders* – agencies will take around 15% commission out of your wages. Some will charge a registration fee – usually between £25 and £70. You'll need to provide the agency with a photo and a CV. Unlike a standard job CV, your supporting artiste CV should focus on your skills and talents – note down whether you can sing, dance or even swim, ride a horse or drive. The more skills you have, the more work you'll get.

The real prize, of course, is to become a successful TV or movie actor. There are two ways of getting in: you can either go to

DAVID TENNANT

KAYA SCODELARIO

drama school, or you can hustle your way in on the strength of your talents, which is pretty much what Johnny Depp did.

If you go to drama school you will be taught the techniques you need to be a professional actor. Crying or laughing to order, for example, can be next to impossible to do convincingly unless you know how. Drama schools will teach you this.

One thing you will need to do is join the actors' union Equity (www.Equity.org.uk). It's difficult to get work in TV or theatre without an Equity card. This is because many broadcasters and stage producers have agreements with Equity. To join, you have to be working professionally or have been offered professional work. Equity also has youth and student branches.

A good place to find acting work is in the "jobs and auditions" section of *The Stage* (www.TheStage.co.uk) newspaper, which comes out every Thursday. It's also worth getting into the casting directory *Spotlight* (www.Spotlight.com) which is used by TV, movie, stage and radio casting-directors to find actors. But you can't get in unless you've got professional experience or recognised academic training.

Another way to get acting work is to find an agent to represent you. They will put you forward for TV, stage and movie auditions. A good place to find an agent is at www.agents-uk.com.

To get into TV and movies you'll need a short film demonstrating your talents. This is known as a "showreel". If you've already got TV or movie experience, you can simply put together three minutes or so of your best performances.

If not, you can create a showreel using a camcorder, or even a webcam at a pinch. You could perform scenes from your favourite movies or theatre plays, talk about an aspect of your life, or sing songs from shows if you happen to have vocal talents.

JOHNNY DEPP

MOVIES

It's not easy to make it as a movie star. It's the jackpot in the world of fame. Consequently, competition is fierce. You really have to fight to get to the top. And as most of the jobs are in Hollywood it will pay you to go and live there.

At first, it's worth taking any job in the movie industry, just to get an idea of how it works and make contacts. You can work as a crew member, or in hair and make-up, wardrobe, or as an extra. Don't forget that many famous actors and actresses got their starts as extras, including Bruce Willis, Dustin Hoffman, Bette Midler, Gary Cooper, Sharon Stone and John Wayne.

To get acting roles you'll need to find an agent and start auditioning. This will get you known to directors and producers. You'll also need to get to know people – other actors, camera crew, literally anyone in the business. The more people you know, the more likely you are to hear about upcoming auditions.

As in music, it's a good idea to set up a MySpace page. Add as many movie industry people as you can to your friends list. Do a photo shoot and put the results on your main page and in the photo albums section. Write an interesting profile and make sure you list at least fifty of your favourite films and books; this helps like-minded people find you.

And if you've got any good videos of you in action, put them on YouTube. It's all about showing off your talents at every opportunity. After all, you never know who might be watching, or when your big break will come.

Studying the craft of acting is also important. Many of the most successful actors have studied at leading drama academies like The New York Film Academy (www.nyfa.com), the Beverly Hills Playhouse (www.bhplayhouse.com), and the Stella Adler Studio of Acting (www.stellaadler.com).

TALENT SHOWS

TV talent shows have always produced stars – going back to *Opportunity Knocks* in the late 1950s. Today, however, many of the biggest talent shows come out of the stable of mega-successful entrepreneur and A&R man Simon Cowell. For singers, of course, the key shows are *The X Factor* (www.xfactor.itv.com) and *American Idol* (www.americanidol.com).

Before you consider auditioning for *The X Factor* or *American Idol*, rehearse the song you plan to perform over and over again. And make sure you know the lyrics off by heart. You should practise what you plan to say to the judges; go over it in front of a mirror. Then record your performance using a camcorder or webcam. Play back your performance and criticise yourself. This will help you iron out any weak points.

Another key thing to bear in mind is that you might be very talented, but you might not be right for *The X Factor* or *American Idol*. Both shows require fairly main-stream sounding singers who have perfect pitch. If your voice is too distinctive, you're unlikely to get beyond the first audition or two.

BRITAIN'S GOT TALENT

ALEXANDRA & CHERYL

Franz Ferdinand frontman Alex Kapranos, for example, doesn't think his band would impress *X Factor* judges Simon Cowell, Dannii Minogue, Cheryl Cole and Louis Walsh. Nor does he think many of today's chart-topping acts would fare well, either.

"We and most of our contemporaries would fail *X Factor* auditions," says the Scottish rocker whose band's hits include "Take Me Out" and "Do You Want To". Alex says he admires the "self-belief" of wannabe stars who put themselves up in front of the judges on the TV talent show.

If you win *The X Factor* or become a close runner-up, a successful career in music is pretty much guaranteed. After being discovered on the show in 2007, classical singer Rhydian Roberts released his first album, *Rhydian*, in November 2008. It went platinum after two weeks, making him the biggest-selling debut male artist of 2008.

Even if you're a runner up on *The X Factor* you can still make the most of your appearance on the show. Consider doing gigs in nightclubs (you'll be the main attraction) and how about contacting large shopping malls to do Saturday afternoon shows? If you did that, you'd also be able to sell CDs and t-shirts.

It's also well worth auditioning for *Britain's Got Talent* (or for *America's Got Talent* if you're in the US). You don't have to be a singer. You can showcase any talent – from dancing and comedy to juggling or gymnastics – so long as it is entertaining. Street dancer George Sampson, for example, won the second series of *Britain's Got Talent* in 2008. He was 14 when he took home the £100,000 prize, and went on to perform at the 2008 Royal Variety Performance, staged at the London Palladium.

Like with *The X Factor* and *American Idol*, the key is to rehearse your act to perfection before auditioning.

DANCE

Becoming a dancer is another great way to get into the public eye. You can appear on TV, in music videos, movies and in stage shows. Even if you've got your sights set on becoming a pop star or actor, being able to dance is a must-have skill in today's entertainment world. "It opens up your scope to get more work," says top choreographer Lynne Page, whose credits include the movie *Billy Elliot* and stage show *Bat Boy – The Musical*.

Lynne has worked with many big stars, including Take That and Dannii Minogue. She says it's crucial to be able to dance if you want to become a star in the world of entertainment. "Ten years ago Gary Barlow of Take That was known as the fat one who couldn't dance," she says. "He could get away with it then, but you can't now. What with the phenomenal success of shows like *Strictly Come Dancing*, you're expected to be able to hold your own as a dancer. If you can't, your gravitas will go out of the window, even if you're a sexy pop star or actor."

The best way to perfect your dance skills is to take classes. Lynne teaches hip-hop and street dancing styles at her dance school Nifty Feet (www.NiftyFeet.com) in London. But you'll be able to find dance workshops in most towns and cities.

If your sights are set on becoming a professional dancer, Lynne recommends taking a three-year course at a vocational dance school. "Some schools will take you at 18, others at 16," she says. "A lot of them are based in London, but not all. You could also try to do dance without training. In rare cases, some people manage to pull this off, but not often."

Check out the following dance schools which offer vocational courses:

★ **Arts Educational Schools London**
www.artsed.co.uk

★ **Doreen Bird College**
www.birdcollege.co.uk

★ **Laine Theatre Arts**
www.laine-theatre-arts.co.uk

★ **Liverpool Institute of Performing Arts (LIPA)** www.lipa.ac.uk

★ **Dance East Academy**
www.danceeast.co.uk/academy

CASE STUDY:
BILLIE PIPER

At only 26, Billie Piper is one of Britain's most successful actresses, most famous for her role as Rose in *Doctor Who*. Born in Swindon, Wiltshire, Billie was called Lianne for the first three weeks of her life before her parents changed it to Billie.

Like a lot of actors and musicians Billie was educated at the Sylvia Young Theatre School in London. Her peers included Amy Winehouse and members of McFly and Busted. Her first foray into the world of entertainment was as a singer. At 15 Billie was signed by Virgin records and her debut single "Because We Want To" stormed into the UK charts at number one, making her one of the youngest singers to have achieved this. She went on to release ten singles and two albums – plus a *Best Of* – before deciding to pursue her acting career.

Despite her success as a singer, Billie isn't sure she'd have cut it had shows like *The X Factor* been around when she started: "I sometimes think, would I have gone on *X Factor*? And no, I wouldn't. I wouldn't have been good enough. These people work so hard and they sing live. I mimed throughout my entire pop career." In 2003, Billie started taking acting lessons in Los Angeles and landed a role in the BBC television series *The Canterbury Tales* – to rave reviews. In 2004, Billie played Orlando Bloom's romantic interest in the film *The Calcium Kid*. She also acted in *Things to do Before You're Thirty* and the horror film *Spirit Trap*.

In 2005, she became a household name when she played Doctor Who's companion Rose Tyler. She went on to win the Most Popular Actress award at the 2005 and 2006 National Television Awards. She has since acted in numerous TV shows including dramatisations of Philip Pullman's books *The Ruby in the Smoke* and *The Shadow of the North*.

CASE STUDY:

JOHNNY DEPP

Most famous for playing the swaggering Jack Sparrow in *The Pirates of the Caribbean* films, Johnny Depp has made quite a name for himself as an actor. Born in Kentucky USA in 1963 to a waitress mum and civil engineer dad, Johnny has a brother and two sisters – one of which, Christy, was his PA, and now works for his film production company.

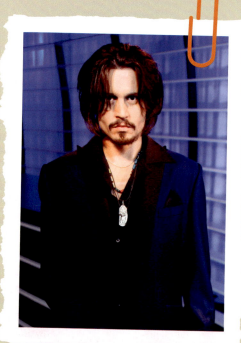

At the age of 12 his mum bought him a guitar and Johnny was hit by the music bug, playing in various garage bands. Aged 20, he married Lori Anne Allison, a make-up artist, who happened to know actor Nicolas Cage. She introduced him to Johnny. Cage thought Johnny had what it takes to be an actor and suggested he give it a go. So he did.

Johnny's first big role was in the 1984 horror movie *Nightmare on Elm Street*. Johnny played the heroine's boyfriend who meets a very sticky end at the hands of Freddy Krueger – aaarrrggghh! He also had numerous TV roles and became something of a teen heart-throb when he appeared in the Fox TV series *21 Jump Street*. But he felt uneasy with this label, saying it was: "A very uncomfortable situation and I didn't get a handle on it and it wasn't on my terms at all."

After this, Johnny vowed only to appear in films he felt were right for him. So began an illustrious career playing mostly off-beat characters such as Edward Scissorhands, Hunter S. Thompson, Willy Wonka in *Charlie and the Chocolate Factory*, and of course, everyone's favourite pirate Jack Sparrow. His latest role is the Mad Hatter in his friend Tim Burton's *Alice in Wonderland*.

HAVE YOU GOT WHAT IT TAKES TO BE A HOLLYWOOD STAR?

QUIZ

1 Are you shy?
A Yes.
B Depends on who I'm with.
C Absolutely not.

2 On school photos are you ...
A The one lurking at the back looking down at your mate's head?
B The one at the side larking around with your mate?
C Sitting dead centre with a radiant grin on your face?

3 Your dad's just got a new camcorder and wants to give it a whirl. Do you ...
A Offer to film him.
B Hover around hoping to get in the shot he's taking of your dog peeing on a neighbour's car.
C Clown around shouting: "Over here, over here. Look at me!"

4 Who do you most admire?
A My parents.
B My teacher/boss – just in case they're reading this.
C Oh, Kate Winslet, Johnny Depp, Steven Spielberg the list goes on ...

ANSWERS

Mostly A's:
Ooh a bit of a shrinking violet – you may be what Hollywood's been waiting for but you need to blow your trumpet a little louder. Get out there and show'em! Try a drama class to bring out the star quality in you.

Mostly B's:
You have the makings of a character actor. You're not over pushy and being on camera doesn't scare you too much. You could start in the background before taking a role as the star's sidekick. Try being a crew member on the next *Pirates* film to start with – then gravitate to something daft like Jack Sparrow's hairdresser!

Mostly C's:
Outta my way Angelina – real talent coming through. You know how to get the attention and you have impeccable self belief. There's a movie with your name on it – you just need to convince Hollywood with your best all singing, all dancing, all dazzling-smile performance.
Good luck!

Got a question? **Ask Jimmy at www.Jimmyleeshreeve.com**

PICTURE CREDITS

Getty: 2, 4, 5, 18, 19, 21, 27, 30, 31, 33, 34, 40, 48, 49, 50, 52, 53 (top)

Rex: 77, 9, 10, 11, 12, 13, 16, 20, 23, 24, 25, 26, 32, 37, 38, 42, 43, 44, 45, 46, 51, 53 (bottom), 54, 56, 57, 59, 60

PA Photos: 6, 8, 14, 15, 22, 35, 36, 39, 55

ACKNOWLEDGEMENTS

Thanks to Jimmy Lee Shreeve, Amanda Harris, Helen Ewing, James Martindale, Jane Sturrock, Frank Brinkley, Daniel Bunyard and Rich Carr.

First published in hardback in Great Britain in 2009 by Orion Books an imprint of the Orion Publishing Group Ltd Orion House, 5 Upper St Martin's Lane, London WC2H 9EA An Hachette Livre UK Company

10 9 8 7 6 5 4 3 2 1

A CIP catalogue record for this book is available from the British Library.

ISBN: 978 1 409 11313 3

Designed by Smith & Gilmour, London
Printed in Spain by Cayfosa

The Orion Publishing Group's policy is to use papers that are natural, renewable and recyclable and made from wood grown in sustainable forests. The logging and manufacturing processes are expected to conform to the environmental regulations of the country of origin.

Every effort has been made to fulfil requirements with regard to reproducing copyright material. The author and publisher will be glad to rectify any omissions at the earliest opportunity.
www.orionbooks.co.uk